HOLYHABITS BIBLE REFLECTIONS | SHARING RESOURCES

The Bible Reading Fellowship
15 The Chambers, Vineyard
Abingdon OX14 3FE
brf.org.uk

The Bible Reading Fellowship (BRF) is a Registered Charity (233280)

ISBN 978 0 85746 835 2
First published 2020
10 9 8 7 6 5 4 3 2 1 0
All rights reserved

Text © individual authors 2020
This edition © The Bible Reading Fellowship 2020
Original design by morsebrowndesign.co.uk & penguinboy.net

The authors assert the moral right to be identified as the authors
of this work

Acknowledgements

Scripture quotations marked NRSV are taken from The New Revised
Standard Version of the Bible, Anglicised edition, copyright © 1989, 1995
by the Division of Christian Education of the National Council of the
Churches of Christ in the United States of America. Used by permission.
All rights reserved.

Scripture quotations marked NIV are taken from The Holy Bible, New
International Version (Anglicised edition) copyright © 1979, 1984, 2011
by Biblica. Used by permission of Hodder & Stoughton Publishers, a
Hachette UK company. All rights reserved. 'NIV' is a registered trademark
of Biblica. UK trademark number 1448790.

Scripture quotations marked KJV are taken from the Authorised Version
of the Bible (The King James Bible), the rights in which are vested in
the Crown, are reproduced by permission of the Crown's Patentee,
Cambridge University Press.

Every effort has been made to trace and contact copyright owners
for material used in this resource. We apologise for any inadvertent
omissions or errors, and would ask those concerned to contact us so that
full acknowledgement can be made in the future.

A catalogue record for this book is available from the British Library

Printed and bound in the UK by Zenith Media NP4 0DQ

SHARING RESOURCES

BIBLE REFLECTIONS
40 READINGS AND REFLECTIONS

Edited by
ANDREW ROBERTS

Contents

Contents

Contents

| George M. Wieland

About the writers

Martin and Margot Hodson: Margot is director of theology and education for the John Ray Initiative (JRI), an organisation connecting environment, science and Christianity, and an Anglican minister in Oxford Diocese. Martin is a plant scientist, environmental biologist and operations director for JRI. The Hodsons have been published widely and have written several books, including *A Christian Guide to Environmental Issues* (BRF, 2015). For more about the Hodsons, see **hodsons.org**.

Veronica Zundel is an Oxford graduate, writer and columnist. She lives with her husband and son in north London. Her most recent book is *Everything I Know about God, I've Learned from Being a Parent* (BRF, 2013).

Chris Pullenayegem is an immigrant of Sri Lankan origin, lives in Canada and grew up in a multireligious and multi-ethnic environment. With an academic background in law, psychology and change leadership and being deeply rooted in theology, Chris brings wisdom, knowledge and skills in assisting congregations to discover and fulfil their God-given role, especially in rapidly changing environments. His expertise lies in church renewal processes, new ministry development, faith formation, policy development and cross-cultural competency training. Chris is a musician and loves the outdoors (when it's warmer).

George M. Wieland is the director of mission research and training at Carey Baptist College, Auckland, New Zealand. He served with his wife Jo in cross-cultural mission, pastored churches in the UK and taught New Testament before taking on his current role, helping to form people for participation in God's mission in our changing world.

Introduction to Holy Habits

> They devoted themselves to the apostles' teaching and fellowship, to the breaking of bread and the prayers. Awe came upon everyone, because many wonders and signs were being done by the apostles. All who believed were together and had all things in common; they would sell their possessions and goods and distribute the proceeds to all, as any had need. Day by day, as they spent much time together in the temple, they broke bread at home and ate their food with glad and generous hearts, praising God and having the goodwill of all the people. And day by day the Lord added to their number those who were being saved.
>
> ACTS 2:42–47 (NRSV)

Holy Habits is a way of forming disciples that is emerging anew from an exploration of this precious portion of scripture, Luke's famous portrait of the early church. As such, it is both deeply biblical and an approach that lives when infused with the life-giving breath of the Holy Spirit – the same Holy Spirit who brought life, energy and creativity to the first Christian communities.

Holy Habits is based upon a series of ten practices that are shown to be fruitful in the Acts 2 passage: biblical teaching, fellowship, breaking bread, prayer, sharing resources, serving, eating together, gladness and generosity, worship, and making more disciples. In this series of material, passages relating to the ten habits are explored one habit at a time, sometimes with reference to other habits. In real life, the habits all get mixed up and complement each other as part of a holistic way of discipleship. You may want to be alert to such connections.

There are many lists in the Bible, and with biblical lists the first and last items often have particular significance. In this list, it is significant that biblical teaching comes first. All of the habits are to be found throughout scripture, and healthy holy habits will be grounded in regular engagement with biblical teaching. This is a foundational habit.

The last habit is also significant. Commentators have remarked that it is no surprise that 'day by day the Lord added to their number' when life was lived in the way Luke describes. Many can be nervous of the word 'evangelism'. Holy Habits offers a way of being evangelistic that may help to assuage some of those nerves.

Holy Habits is a way of life for followers of Jesus individually and collectively. In Acts 2:42–47, Luke offers clues as to how these practices can be fruitful. Note the devotion he mentions at the beginning and the repeated use of the word 'all'. Holy Habits is a way of life for all ages (including children), cultures and contexts. The habits are to be lived day by day, in the whole of life, Monday to Saturday as well as Sunday. And note how Luke attributes the growth that results to the Lord. These are *holy* habits, which flourish when the Lord is at the centre of all.

Introduction to Sharing Resources

The picture of church that Luke presents in Acts 2:42–47 and Acts 4:32–37 is often described as a 'community of goods'. It is simultaneously an inspiring and a challenging picture and one full of hope in these days of great uncertainty in our world.

In his commentary on Acts, James Dunn writes that Luke's picture may be 'somewhat idealised' (*The Acts of the Apostles*, Epworth 1996, p. 34), so we do need to handle the picture with care. But having said that, we are nowhere without ideals, and Dunn goes on to say that anyone familiar with movements of spiritual renewal will recognise 'authentic notes' in the picture that Luke presents, including 'the readiness for unreserved commitment to one another in a shared common life'.

The way of living that Luke describes is one to be practised within our church communities but not limited to them. Most modern economies are run on models of growth which assume that there will be a never-ending supply of increasing resources. This model is sold to consumers, who then behave in accord with these assumptions, constantly striving for more. This way of thinking is being challenged with increasing urgency, as the realisation grows that there is not a never-ending supply of resources and that consumption of these resources is putting the future of the planet in great danger.

Against this background, Luke's picture of a community that shares its resources and gives to any according to their need is powerfully prophetic. This is a picture to inform and shape our shopping, voting and attitudes to taxation, our relationships and our engagement with the big issues of our times. In these reflections, you will find the writers inviting you to reflect on these things. In George Wieland's material, you will find helpful reflections on the *how* of sharing our resources and the spirit of giving.

Giving is a key part of God's nature, and it is possible to read the Bible as a narrative of giving. In Genesis, we see God gifting creation to humanity (Genesis 1:26–31; 2:16–25). It is not long before selfishness (sin) damages the gift and the relationships that were designed to let life flourish. But this does not stop God giving. Resources continue to be given through the mundane and the miraculous. Wisdom, teaching and prophecy are given to guide holy living. Then, in the climactic words of John's gospel, 'God so loved the world that he gave his only Son, so that everyone who believes in him may not perish but may have eternal life' (John 3:16, NRSV).

Even when this gift is rejected, God keeps on giving – giving new life to Jesus, who had been crucified by the selfishness of sin, and giving the gift of the Spirit at Pentecost which birthed the 'community of goods'. So when it comes to thinking about the holy habit of sharing resources, we need to always locate that thinking within the generous and persistent giving of God.

| Martin and Margot Hodson

Stewardship

Genesis 1:28–30

God blessed them and said to them, 'Be fruitful and increase in number; fill the earth and subdue it. Rule over the fish in the sea and the birds in the sky and over every living creature that moves on the ground.' Then God said, 'I give you every seed-bearing plant on the face of the whole earth and every tree that has fruit with seed in it. They will be yours for food. And to all the beasts of the earth and all the birds in the sky and all the creatures that move along the ground – everything that has the breath of life in it – I give every green plant for food.' And it was so.   (NIV)

| Reflection |

How should we relate to nature? The command to 'fill the earth and subdue it' is controversial. In the King James Version our passage reads, 'Have dominion over the fish...' Words like subdue and dominion can seem very harsh, and down the ages people, including Christians, have used passages like this as excuses to do what they like with creation. Famously, in 1967, this led American historian Lynn White Jr to state that 'Christianity is the most anthropocentric religion the world has seen'.

Since White launched his attack, biblical scholars have looked more closely at the Hebrew words in this passage. It seems that the word used for 'subdue' is possibly a ploughing metaphor, which suggests aiding the fruitfulness of the land rather than treading it down. The word we translate 'dominion' or 'rule' is the same word as that used by King Solomon in his just reign over Israel. So the original Hebrew meaning of the passage was almost certainly not as harsh as it has often been interpreted. In fact, this passage has more recently been used to support a positive ethical view.

White's attack on Christianity and its attitude to the natural world set in motion a whole train of thinking and stimulated the development of environmental ethics and theology. Our passage and others like it were used to develop the concept of stewardship, the idea that humans are responsible for the world and should take care of it. But stewardship soon went beyond thinking about the natural world. It is now often applied to money and in financial and business affairs. If we are thinking about how we share our resources, then we are really thinking about stewardship.

> Lord God, give me wisdom as we look at the topic of sharing resources in this series. Amen

Martin and Margot Hodson

| Martin and Margot Hodson

Hospitality

Genesis 18:1–5

The Lord appeared to Abraham near the great trees of Mamre while he was sitting at the entrance to his tent in the heat of the day. Abraham looked up and saw three men standing nearby. When he saw them, he hurried from the entrance of his tent to meet them and bowed low to the ground. He said, 'If I have found favour in your eyes, my lord, do not pass your servant by. Let a little water be brought, and then you may all wash your feet and rest under this tree. Let me get you something to eat, so you can be refreshed and then go on your way – now that you have come to your servant.' 'Very well,' they answered, 'do as you say.'

(NIV)

Reflection

Genesis 18 opens in a somewhat mysterious way, when three men appear to Abraham as he rested at the entrance of his tent on a hot day. Abraham somehow recognises that one of them is the Lord (the other two may have been angels) and immediately offers them hospitality, first water to drink and to wash their feet and later a meal. This kind of hospitality was, and still is, typical of that found in the Middle East. The New Testament church was also very much built on hospitality and takes up this theme in 1 Peter 4:9: 'Offer hospitality to one another without grumbling.'

Years ago, I (Martin) was between houses and staying in a small bedsit until a house purchase went through six weeks later. There were no cooking facilities. I was working at Birmingham University and so food was no problem in the week, and I spied out the fish and chip shop for Sunday lunch. But I also spotted the small local church and went there on my first Sunday. After the service, at coffee, an older couple came up to me, recognising that I was new. Would I like lunch? When I got to their house, they had lots of guests for lunch. They had food on the go every week, never knowing who the guests would be! When I explained my situation, they fixed me up with Sunday lunch every week with a different church family. I never needed the chip shop. Whenever I hear the word 'hospitality', it always takes me back to that small church.

Sharing hospitality, especially food, is a key biblical principle. It is perhaps not surprising that many modern church initiatives (e.g. Alpha and Messy Church) also involve sharing a meal together.

> Lord, give me opportunities to help my church develop its ministry of hospitality. Amen

Martin and Margot Hodson

Tithing

Deuteronomy 14:22–23, 28–29

Be sure to set aside a tenth of all that your fields produce each year. Eat the tithe of your corn, new wine and olive oil, and the firstborn of your herds and flocks in the presence of the Lord your God at the place he will choose as a dwelling for his Name, so that you may learn to revere the Lord your God always... At the end of every three years, bring all the tithes of that year's produce and store it in your towns, so that the Levites (who have no land allotted to them or inheritance of their own) and the foreigners, the fatherless and the widows who live in your towns may come and eat and be satisfied, and so that the Lord your God may bless you in all the work of your hands.

(NIV)

Reflection

From the first part of this passage, it is clear that the original command to the Jewish people concerning tithing suggested that they should put aside a tenth of their agricultural produce each year and then eat it in a place chosen by God. In the second section, we see that every three years tithes were to be used to support the Levites who worked at the temple and the poor and vulnerable. Throughout the Old Testament, tithing is a strong theme, and this is carried over into the New Testament when Jesus states, 'Woe to you, teachers of the law and Pharisees, you hypocrites! You give a tenth of your spices – mint, dill and cumin. But you have neglected the more important matters of the law – justice, mercy and faithfulness. You should have practised the latter, without neglecting the former' (Matthew 23:23).

Throughout history, churches have had various regulations concerning tithing, some voluntary and some compulsory. Most gifts are now in the form of money. But how do we decide where our money should go? Clearly the provision for the Levites gives a strong precedent for the support of the church and its ministers, and without our support the institutions would flounder and our clergy would not be able to undertake full-time ministry. However, Jesus makes it evident that giving should come from the heart and not just be a mechanical process. So 'justice, mercy and faithfulness' also come into tithing. There are very many worthy charities working with the poor and homeless that could really do with our help. We need to prayerfully consider where we place our giving. Many Christians give a certain percentage to their church, and the rest to the charities they particularly support. Maybe that could be a way forward for you?

Lord, show me how to apportion my giving. Amen

| Martin and Margot Hodson

Justice

Deuteronomy 15:1–5

At the end of every seven years you must cancel debts. This is how it is to be done: every creditor shall cancel any loan they have made to a fellow Israelite. They shall not require payment from anyone among their own people, because the Lord's time for cancelling debts has been proclaimed. You may require payment from a foreigner, but you must cancel any debt your fellow Israelite owes you. However, there need be no poor people among you, for in the land the Lord your God is giving you to possess as your inheritance, he will richly bless you, if only you fully obey the Lord your God and are careful to follow all these commands I am giving you today.

(NIV)

Reflection

The premise that every seven years the Israelites should cancel their debts is related to the idea of sabbath, as expressed in Genesis 2:2 when God rested from his creative activity. This is then extended to giving the land a sabbath: 'During the seventh year let the land lie unploughed and unused' (Exodus 23:11). In carrying out this command, the Israelites would in effect be repaying their debt to the land and giving it a rest. Our passage today extends this idea to the people. They should be free of debt, and God intended that there should be no poor people among them. Paul has this to say about debt: 'Let no debt remain outstanding, except the continuing debt to love one another, for whoever loves others has fulfilled the law' (Romans 13:8).

Despite all these good intentions, people are still in debt, as indeed are whole countries. Although there are fewer poor people in the world now than at the turn of the millennium, globally inequality has grown, with a few very rich people having more wealth than millions of poor people. As our passage and many others in the Bible make clear, God is a God of justice, and he cares about the poor and those who are in debt.

Throughout history, Christians have taken up this theme, trying to 'transform unjust structures of society', as the fourth of the Anglican marks of mission puts it. Jubilee 2000 sought to relieve poor countries of crippling debts which prevented them from developing. More recent campaigns include Drop the Debt and Make Poverty History. In all these cases, Christians were very much involved, often taking leading positions. How can we help? We can give assistance to finance organisations working in this area, we can write to our politicians and we can get directly involved in this work as individuals and as churches.

> God of justice, how can I help 'transform unjust structures of society'?

Generosity

Deuteronomy 15:7–10

If anyone is poor among your fellow Israelites in any of the towns of the land that the Lord your God is giving you, do not be hard-hearted or tight-fisted towards them. Rather, be open-handed and freely lend them whatever they need. Be careful not to harbour this wicked thought: 'The seventh year, the year for cancelling debts, is near,' so that you do not show ill will towards the needy among your fellow Israelites and give them nothing. They may then appeal to the Lord against you, and you will be found guilty of sin. Give generously to them and do so without a grudging heart; then because of this the Lord your God will bless you in all your work and in everything you put your hand to. (NIV)

Reflection

Although our previous passage suggested that the ideal was that there would be no poor people in Israel, God is realistic and knows that there will be. So how are we to treat these people? Here and throughout the Bible, we are instructed to give generously. But how this should be done raises all sorts of issues. Jesus gives this advice: 'But when you give to the needy, do not let your left hand know what your right hand is doing, so that your giving may be in secret. Then your Father, who sees what is done in secret, will reward you' (Matthew 6:3–4). It is clear that we should not be making a lot of our giving, and preferably this should be done in secret.

But what do we do today when we pass someone begging in the street? There are two main approaches. We could stop and give the person some money directly. The disadvantage of this is that we do not know what the money will be used for. Giving money can exacerbate any problems with addiction, which interact with homelessness. The other route is to give money to organisations that are working with the beggars and the homeless. These will have specialist knowledge and will be able to ensure that any money given is well used. It still feels hard, though, walking past people. It may be that different approaches are appropriate depending on the circumstances. The most important thing is to acknowledge people, to say hello and maybe offer some food. Some homeless shelters offer tokens that people can buy to give out. Whatever route we eventually decide to take, we should 'not show ill will towards the needy' and give generously to those less well off than ourselves.

> Lord, give me a spirit of generosity. Amen

Martin and Margot Hodson

Gleaning

Deuteronomy 24:19–22

When you are harvesting in your field and you overlook a sheaf, do not go back to get it. Leave it for the foreigner, the fatherless and the widow, so that the Lord your God may bless you in all the work of your hands. When you beat the olives from your trees, do not go over the branches a second time. Leave what remains for the foreigner, the fatherless and the widow. When you harvest the grapes in your vineyard, do not go over the vines again. Leave what remains for the foreigner, the fatherless and the widow. Remember that you were slaves in Egypt. That is why I command you to do this. (NIV)

Martin and Margot Hodson

Reflection

Years ago, an old Cotswold farmer was asked why he did not shoot the rabbits in his wheat field. His response was that he harvested 90% of the wheat and he left the rest to his rabbits. He may or may not have realised it, but he was following a biblical principle, in that he was allowing the rabbits to glean his fields.

In the Bible, gleaning is the collection of grain, grapes and other crops left behind after the main harvest. So the Cotswold farmer was even more generous, as he didn't mind his rabbits gathering some of the wheat even before it was harvested. Gleaning was intended to be kind to poor people and to foreigners. Our passage calls on the Jewish people to 'remember that you were slaves in Egypt' and to do justice. Perhaps the most famous story of gleaning in the Bible concerns Ruth the Moabite (Ruth 2). Ruth and Naomi were almost certainly very hungry after a long journey from Moab to Israel, so Ruth went gleaning barley in a field. There she met the owner of the field, Boaz, who was very kind to her and eventually married her. And so Ruth the Moabite became the great-grandmother of King David.

Where do we see the principle of gleaning being applied today? It is still best seen in an agricultural context. For many years now, farmers have been able to apply for Environmental Stewardship schemes in the UK. These help nature to flourish by careful management practices. So we often see wild flower strips around the edges of fields. The farmers allow nature to glean from their fields and share their resources with the rich biodiversity that can develop. In return, the insects resident in the strips often help protect the fields against pests.

How might you apply the principle of gleaning in your life?

> Dear God, show me how to leave a little of my bounty for other people and/or other creatures. Amen

| Martin and Margot Hodson

Food

1 Kings 17:13–16

Elijah said to her, 'Don't be afraid. Go home and do as you have said. But first make a small loaf of bread for me from what you have and bring it to me, and then make something for yourself and your son. For this is what the Lord, the God of Israel, says: "The jar of flour will not be used up and the jug of oil will not run dry until the day the Lord sends rain on the land."' She went away and did as Elijah had told her. So there was food every day for Elijah and for the woman and her family. For the jar of flour was not used up and the jug of oil did not run dry, in keeping with the word of the Lord spoken by Elijah.

(NIV)

Reflection

The story of Elijah and the widow at Zarephath takes place in the context of a severe drought in Israel which lasted for several years. After being fed by the ravens, Elijah was instructed by God to go to Zarephath, where a widow would give him food. When he arrived there, he found her gathering sticks to make a fire. She intended to use her last remaining flour and oil to make a meal for her and her son before they both died from starvation. Elijah asked God for a miracle that would keep himself, the widow and her son in bread and oil until the end of the famine. This is the first miracle involving multiplication of food recorded in the Bible.

There are many places in the world where people are going hungry today. Sadly, there are now many in the United Kingdom who do not have enough food to eat. The response of the churches across the country has been amazing, with many involved in setting up food banks. The Trussell Trust, a Christian charity, has become the largest provider of food banks. According to their statistics, 658,048 emergency supplies were provided to people between April and September 2018, a 13% increase on the same period in 2017. Families with children are those most likely to need food banks, and there are many reports in the media of children going without food.

What can we do about this crisis? How can we share our resources? Food banks are always looking for volunteers. Churches can set up or help run food banks in more deprived areas. In well-off areas, food can be collected and taken to towns and cities where the need is greater. Be careful to be on the lookout for food poverty, even in places that appear to be wealthy. And pray.

> Lord, show me how I can help the hungry in my community.
> Amen

Martin and Margot Hodson

Interest

2 Kings 4:1–3

The wife of a man from the company of the prophets cried out to Elisha, 'Your servant my husband is dead, and you know that he revered the Lord. But now his creditor is coming to take my two boys as his slaves.' Elisha replied to her, 'How can I help you? Tell me, what do you have in your house?' 'Your servant has nothing there at all,' she said, 'except a small jar of olive oil.' Elisha said, 'Go round and ask all your neighbours for empty jars. Don't ask for just a few.' (NIV)

Reflection

The Bible is not keen on the charging of interest on loans. God does not like debt and wants to help people that are in such trouble. In today's passage, we hear the story of a woman whose husband has recently died, and his creditors are threatening to take her sons into slavery if she does not pay off his debts. Elisha asks her what she owns, and she says she just has one small jar of olive oil. The prophet says she should ask her neighbours for more empty jars. She should then pour oil into them. The oil from the one small jar filled many others – a miracle! The woman then sold the oil and was able to pay off her debts.

Throughout history, loans for interest have been controversial and often criticised. According to the Jewish commentator Rashi, the Hebrew word for 'bite' has the same root as the word for 'interest': 'It resembles the bite of a snake… inflicting a small wound in a person's foot which he does not feel at first, but all at once it swells, and distends the whole body up to the top of his head. So it is with interest.'

Today, people still get into debt and struggle with high-interest payments. In 2013, the Archbishop of Canterbury, Justin Welby, launched an attack on the payday loan companies operating in the UK. These companies were charging very high interest rates, and desperate people were trapped in a cycle of debt. Three years later, tougher regulations have forced many of the companies out of business, but debt remains a very serious problem. Many churches have responded to the debt crisis by setting up schemes to give monetary advice. Often there are people in their congregations who are real experts in financial affairs who are willing to help.

Lord God, I pray for all those trapped in debt.
Show me how I might be able to help. Amen

Martin and Margot Hodson

Famine

2 Kings 4:38–41

Elisha returned to Gilgal and there was a famine in that region. While the company of the prophets was meeting with him, he said to his servant, 'Put on the large pot and cook some stew for these prophets.' One of them went out into the fields to gather herbs and found a wild gourd plant and picked as many of its gourds as his garment could hold. When he returned, he cut them up into the pot of stew, though no one knew what they were. The stew was poured out for the men, but as they began to eat it, they cried out, 'Man of God, there is death in the pot!' And they could not eat it. Elisha said, 'Get some flour.' He put it into the pot and said, 'Serve it to the people to eat.' And there was nothing harmful in the pot.

(NIV)

Martin and Margot Hodson

Reflection

This is a rather mysterious story! In the midst of a famine, Elisha was trying to be hospitable to a group of prophets that had gathered around him. He sent his servant off to find some vegetables. The servant spotted a wild vine and grabbed as many of its gourds as he could carry. What exactly was the gourd plant? It seems that it was colocynth (*Citrullus colocynthis*), a vine that trails along the sand in the desert near the Dead Sea. The plant is used in traditional medicines, including as a laxative, but it is toxic and potentially fatal. Colocynth was said to have been used by Agrippina to poison her husband, the Roman Emperor Claudius, in AD54. Not surprisingly, the bitter taste of the stew, and some of the early symptoms of eating a small amount of it, provoked a negative reaction from the prophets: 'There is death in the pot!' Elisha solved the problem by adding flour to the stew. This would surely have decreased the bitter taste, but why the stew suddenly lost its toxicity is not certain. Maybe it was a miracle?

Hunger and famine are still major problems. The second of the Sustainable Development Goals, set by the United Nations in 2015, is 'Zero Hunger'. They estimated that 815 million people were undernourished, mostly in poor countries. The ambitious aim is that by 2030 nobody should be hungry. Reaching this target at a time of rapid population growth, climate change and biodiversity loss, and without wrecking our agricultural soils, will be a major challenge. Only a few people will have the necessary skills to help the United Nations achieve this laudable goal in a direct way. But there are many secular and Christian charities that are working in this area. You could support one or more of these as an individual and encourage your church to do the same.

> Lord Jesus, I pray that there will soon come a time when nobody in the world goes hungry. Amen

Martin and Margot Hodson

Compassion

Exodus 22:25–27

> If you lend money to one of my people among you who is needy, do not treat it like a business deal; charge no interest. If you take your neighbour's cloak as a pledge, return it by sunset, because that cloak is the only covering your neighbour has. What else can they sleep in? When they cry out to me, I will hear, for I am compassionate.
>
> (NIV)

| Martin and Margot Hodson

Reflection

If a person got into debt, the Jewish law said that under some circumstances they could make a pledge. So in our present passage, a person gets into debt to a neighbour and loses his cloak as a pledge or surety. But because the person is poor, the neighbour is supposed to return it to him every night to sleep in. In practice, continually having to pick up the cloak in the morning and return it in the evening would probably have put the neighbour off doing so. God is a God of mercy and compassion and listens to the cries of the people, particularly the poor.

Neil deGrasse Tyson, the American scientist and media personality, once said, 'For me, I am driven by two main philosophies: know more today about the world than I knew yesterday and lessen the suffering of others. You'd be surprised how far that gets you.' As a scientist, it is Tyson's job to increase our knowledge of the world. But it is all of our jobs to be compassionate and to lessen suffering. How are we to do that? We have seen that there are many ways we can help. We can carefully consider the stewardship of our financial resources, and help others with how they look after money. We can offer hospitality. We can support charities that help with the homeless on our streets, help to feed the hungry both close to home and across the world, and fight against injustice wherever we see it. And don't forget that we need to share our resources with the rest of creation – leave a bit at the edge of our fields for our rabbits!

> Pray for wisdom. God says, 'I will hear, for I am compassionate.' Amen

| Veronica Zundel

Thought for food

2 Kings 4:42–44

A man came from Baal-shalishah, bringing food from the first fruits to the man of God: twenty loaves of barley and fresh ears of grain in his sack. Elisha said, 'Give it to the people and let them eat.' But his servant said, 'How can I set this before a hundred people?' So he repeated, 'Give it to the people and let them eat, for thus says the Lord, "They shall eat and have some left."' He set it before them, they ate, and had some left, according to the word of the Lord.

(NRSV)

| Veronica Zundel

Reflection

In the stories of Elijah and Elisha, there are several accounts of miraculous feeding – does this one remind you of anything in the New Testament? Jesus' feeding of hungry crowds positions him firmly as a prophet who performs signs, as well as giving teaching and challenges.

As the daughter of a Jewish mother, it is easy for me to see food as love. The hospitality of the meal table is the most basic form of sharing resources there is. Everyone needs to eat, and to eat together (another holy habit) is to form a bond that few other activities can achieve. Like the stories of Jesus feeding a crowd, this one begins with just one person's relatively small offering and ends with everyone being satisfied and there being food left over – suggesting the opportunity to invite even more.

Sikh gurdwaras, or temples, cook food every day for sharing with the homeless or the lonely. My husband helps at a centre run by the London Catholic Worker community that houses and feeds destitute male asylum seekers (they have a similar centre for women and children at a farm in Hertfordshire). Local shops and restaurants donate all the food. It may not meet the standards of supermarkets in terms of how it looks, but it is perfectly nutritious and much appreciated. The cooks are the members of the Catholic Worker community and volunteers from other churches.

One church I heard of had the slogan 'No meeting together without eating together'. Jesus put a meal at the heart of our remembering him.

How can your church or other Christian group place hospitality at the heart of its life?

| Veronica Zundel

Eating with the enemy

Psalm 23

The Lord is my shepherd, I shall not want. He makes me lie down in green pastures; he leads me beside still waters; he restores my soul. He leads me in right paths for his name's sake. Even though I walk through the darkest valley, I fear no evil; for you are with me; your rod and your staff – they comfort me. You prepare a table before me in the presence of my enemies; you anoint my head with oil; my cup overflows. Surely goodness and mercy shall follow me all the days of my life, and I shall dwell in the house of the Lord my whole life long.

(NRSV)

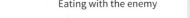

Reflection

Some Bible passages are so familiar that we don't really notice them anymore. It's only on rereading this that I have noticed a new possibility. I always thought of the psalmist eating in defiance of his enemies. But what if the table God prepares for him is in fact an invitation to his enemies to join him in a meal of friendship? This would connect well to the stories Jesus tells of a king giving a banquet and inviting random people off the street to join him, and is in stark contrast to some sects where those who disagree refuse to eat with each other.

A friend of mine works in restorative justice. In this approach, those who have committed crimes meet their victims in order to see the impact of their actions, apologise and be reconciled. It can be far more effective than mere punishment – and it is certainly a way of putting into practice the command to love our enemies.

It is not easy to sit down and share food, or emotions, with someone who has harmed you – or even with someone you have harmed. But it can transform relationships and bring healing. When Jesus tells us to treat someone who has offended us 'as a Gentile and a tax collector' (Matthew 18:17), he surely did not mean us to shun them – after all, he did not shun such outcasts himself. Surely he meant we should show them the love of God.

> What resources could you share in order to be reconciled with an enemy? Might they include the resources of forgiveness?

| Veronica Zundel

What goes around, comes around

Proverbs 11:16–17, 24–26; 19:17

A gracious woman gets honour, but she who hates virtue is covered with shame. The timid become destitute, but the aggressive gain riches. Those who are kind reward themselves, but the cruel do themselves harm... Some give freely, yet grow all the richer; others withhold what is due, and only suffer want. A generous person will be enriched, and one who gives water will get water. The people curse those who hold back grain, but a blessing is on the head of those who sell it... Whoever is kind to the poor lends to the Lord, and will be repaid in full. (NRSV)

Reflection

Biblical proverbs are aimed both to tell us about how life is and to help us see how it could be. So we may observe as a fact that those who seek wealth generally gain it, and that the less pushy may be left behind. But this passage also holds out a different option: that in sharing, we actually gain more than we ever give. Even on a national and local level, our taxes allow us to have the public services we need. And the individual philanthropist, who shares what they have been given, is generally loved. On the negative side, those who give little or nothing may be socially isolated and little liked.

When the diocese I was in many years ago surveyed giving in its churches, it found that the poorer the parish, the more it gave per head. Something about being economically comfortable can make us forget to share. In general, we will find great generosity among poor societies, and sometimes we need to learn to receive as well as give.

I find particularly fascinating the idea that to give to the needy is to lend to God. If we lend money to a friend, we expect to be paid back, perhaps even with interest. Micro-credit schemes allow us to lend to would-be entrepreneurs in developing countries – and when we are repaid, we can lend again. But to lend to God is to put no limits on what we might receive back – not necessarily in money, but in blessing and peace.

When have you experienced generosity from those who had little? When have you given, and received more back?

| Veronica Zundel

Business and charity

Proverbs 31:15–20

She rises while it is still night and provides food for her household and tasks for her servant-girls. She considers a field and buys it; with the fruit of her hands she plants a vineyard. She girds herself with strength, and makes her arms strong. She perceives that her merchandise is profitable. Her lamp does not go out at night. She puts her hands to the distaff, and her hands hold the spindle. She opens her hand to the poor, and reaches out her hands to the needy.

(NRSV)

| Veronica Zundel

Reflection

The first thing we need to remember about the 'ideal woman' of Proverbs 31 is that she is fictional. And the second is that she was probably invented by a man! She has been used too often to beat real women over the head.

Notice, however, that she is an accomplished businesswoman, managing her staff, a canny shopper (or perhaps farmer), a landowner and someone who practises useful crafts to provide clothing for others and herself. What she does not do is hoard for herself the wealth she creates. She does not use 'charity begins at home' as an excuse not to help outsiders. Instead, she recognises that while it may begin at home, it does not end there.

Women are still at the heart of much charitable and voluntary work. Now that most of us are still relatively fit and well at retirement, there is a vast potential workforce who have the time and willingness to help those in need. In the Bruderhof, a Christian residential community I have had contact with, the older members do not retire, but are given jobs to suit their strength and experience. As a result, they don't feel useless or set aside.

What about if we are still pulled various ways by the needs of work and family – perhaps squeezed between looking after a younger and an older generation? We can still support projects run by our church or other voluntary organisations, by our prayers and perhaps by financial giving. And we can join in with whatever capacity we have. The point is not to feel guilty if we cannot give much, but to be part of a more generous society.

> Pray that God will show you where you can share,
> even if only in a limited way.

| Veronica Zundel

Breaking the yoke

Isaiah 58:6–9a

Is not this the fast that I choose: to loose the bonds of injustice, to undo the thongs of the yoke, to let the oppressed go free, and to break every yoke? Is it not to share your bread with the hungry, and bring the homeless poor into your house; when you see the naked, to cover them, and not to hide yourself from your own kin? Then your light shall break forth like the dawn, and your healing shall spring up quickly; your vindicator shall go before you, the glory of the Lord shall be your rearguard. Then you shall call, and the Lord will answer; you shall cry for help, and he will say, Here I am.   (NRSV)

Reflection

Yokes are of two kinds. One yokes together two animals to pull a vehicle; the other is an individual yoke, designed to help someone carry a load (think of a traditional milkmaid carrying churns). Both are designed to make a burdensome task easier. But in this prophecy, Isaiah suggests our calling is not simply to ease the lives of those yoked to hard labour; it is to take away the yoke altogether. This suggests to me that our kingdom calling is not charity, helpful though that may be, but justice.

Charity can be performed without radically altering the status quo. Justice demands political campaigning, challenging the powers that be. Some are called to do this within the machinery of government, as MPs or local councillors. Others stand outside the court and act for change in the structures that keep people unequal. Both work best when many people work together – a different, more liberating way of being yoked. It is worth noting that Isaiah's call here is a corporate one to the people of Israel, not to isolated individuals. Jubilee Debt Campaign, for instance, has both challenged and worked with government to free developing countries from unjust indebtedness. Churches have had a key role in the movement.

Historically, Christians have been at the forefront of issues like the abolition of slavery, reform of prisons and extending education to all. We can still be at the vanguard of social reform, not lagging behind the wider society.

Is there an unjust yoke that particularly concerns you or your church?

| Veronica Zundel

A different inheritance

Matthew 25:34–36

(Then the king will say to those at his right hand, "Come, you that are blessed by my Father, inherit the kingdom prepared for you from the foundation of the world; for I was hungry and you gave me food, I was thirsty and you gave me something to drink, I was a stranger and you welcomed me, I was naked and you gave me clothing, I was sick and you took care of me, I was in prison and you visited me.'"

(NRSV)

Reflection

It took me many years of reading and rereading this passage before I noticed that in this parable, Jesus portrays the king as calling not individuals but 'the nations' before him for judgement. This both lifts burdens of individual guilt and inadequacy and also brings a new challenge to government and society, to care for its weakest and most oppressed.

This does not take away individual responsibility to share, however. I have long admired those such as the Australian missionaries Dave and Ange Andrews, who opened their home to drug addicts, those with AIDS and other marginalised people in the name of Jesus. They realised very soon that the only effective way to heal the broken, without becoming broken oneself, was to do it in community with others with the same call.

Another hero of mine is the late God's Squad founder John Smith, who moved from a very conservative church background to work among biker gangs, introducing them to the Jesus who also chose to be at the edge of society. His life demonstrates that sharing with those in need, whether spiritual or physical need (often both), may demand moving outside our comfort zone, even becoming someone we never thought we could be.

The word 'inherit' stands out for me here. Many of us have inherited a relatively privileged life in world terms. But to gain an eternal inheritance, we may need to let go of that privilege or at least be prepared to share it with others less advantaged.

Pray for anyone you know who is short of food, ill or involved in crime – and for those who work to help them, both at the individual and at the political level. In addition to the resources of prayer, what other resources might you share with them?

| Veronica Zundel

Greed is not good

Mark 10:21–25

Jesus, looking at him, loved him and said, 'You lack one thing; go, sell what you own, and give the money to the poor, and you will have treasure in heaven; then come, follow me.' When he heard this, he was shocked and went away grieving, for he had many possessions. Then Jesus looked around and said to his disciples, 'How hard it will be for those who have wealth to enter the kingdom of God!' And the disciples were perplexed at these words. But Jesus said to them again, 'Children, how hard it is to enter the kingdom of God! It is easier for a camel to go through the eye of a needle than for someone who is rich to enter the kingdom of God.'

(NRSV)

Reflection

Why were the disciples perplexed? We know this story, so we know what's coming at the end. But for Jesus' first followers, personal wealth was a sign of righteousness, a reward for good behaviour. Jesus, however, turns the thinking of his day on its head. Wealth is an obstacle to entering God's kingdom.

These are not easy words for those of us in the affluent west to hear. We often define ourselves by what we own, and it can get in the way of radical dependence on God. The kingdom is a place of sharing, and the more we have, the less willing we may be to share.

The Freecycle Network, Freegle and other online sharing platforms, as well as charity shops, can help us give away surplus possessions or gain things we need without spending on new products. We could also engage in more sharing in our churches. Why does every family in the church need, for instance, a particular household gadget when a few could have one and lend it out? Why not run a toy library for children?

At bottom, this is a spiritual issue. If all our security is in possessions, what need do we have of God or of each other? I need to hear this myself, for I struggle to live more simply. My only hope is: 'Jesus, looking at him, loved him.'

How can you become less dependent on things you own?

| Veronica Zundel

Rip-off religion?

Mark 12:41–44

> [Jesus] sat down opposite the treasury, and watched the crowd putting money into the treasury. Many rich people put in large sums. A poor widow came and put in two small copper coins, which are worth a penny. Then he called his disciples and said to them, 'Truly I tell you, this poor widow has put in more than all those who are contributing to the treasury. For all of them have contributed out of their abundance; but she out of her poverty has put in everything she had, all she had to live on.' (NRSV)

Reflection

The usual understanding of this story is that Jesus is praising the widow for her sacrificial giving. But a commentary I read many years ago takes a very different angle. Right before this episode Jesus condemns the scribes who 'devour widows' houses', and right after, he predicts the destruction of the temple and all it stands for. So is it possible that rather than praising the widow, he is exposing how much the religious system of the day exploits the poor and faithful? The rich give to the treasury out of their surplus, but when the widow has given the smallest offering possible, she will still have to miss her next meal and maybe several more.

'Ah, but that was then,' you may say. 'Our religious institutions don't exploit people today.' Think, however, of the televangelists who grow rich on the donations of those who can ill afford to give, but who are promised healing or blessing or even wealth if they do. Not so much has changed.

What does this say to us about sharing? Surely it reminds us that those who have received most (and that, in global terms, is most of us in the west) are called to give most. John Wesley set a budget of £28 for his annual living expenses (that was a fair income in his day) and gave away everything else he earned, up to thousands of pounds. What if we, too, regarded everything but what covers our basic needs as belonging to God, not to us?

> Do we ever, in our preaching or conversation, demand sacrifices of others that we are not prepared to make ourselves?

Walking the walk

Luke 3:7–11

> John said to the crowds that came out to be baptised by him, 'You brood of vipers! Who warned you to flee from the wrath to come? Bear fruits worthy of repentance. Do not begin to say to yourselves, "We have Abraham as our ancestor"; for I tell you, God is able from these stones to raise up children to Abraham. Even now the axe is lying at the root of the trees; every tree therefore that does not bear good fruit is cut down and thrown into the fire.' And the crowds asked him, 'What then should we do?' In reply he said to them, 'Whoever has two coats must share with anyone who has none; and whoever has food must do likewise.' (NRSV)

Reflection

John the Baptist's calling was to prepare people for the coming of Jesus. So what was his approach? Did he carefully explain the doctrines of the incarnation and the atonement? Did he invite people to ensure their place in heaven? No, he challenged, indeed positively insulted, his followers, who were perhaps merely looking for the latest religious trend. Repentance was not enough, he declared; it was only worthwhile if 'fruit', or acts of righteousness, followed. And the people clearly understood what he was saying: they asked not 'What then should we believe?' but 'What then should we do?'

Following Jesus is primarily a way of living and only secondarily a set of beliefs. Sharing is at the very heart of this lifestyle: if you have good things to spare, give them away to those who have none.

I confess I find this hard. I haven't counted the number of coats I have, but it's a lot more than two! It is easy to give away things you don't really need or aren't particularly attached to. It is harder to part with our favourites. But it is something we need to learn. Some towns have started schemes where, for instance, scarves are tied round trees, or clothes racks placed in town centres with coats hung on them, for the homeless or cash-strapped to take. Sadly, one of these coatracks was recently vandalised. Living differently may not make us popular.

> How could you and your fellow church members encourage each other to live simply and share more?

| Veronica Zundel

Freely you have received

Luke 6:32–36

'If you love those who love you, what credit is that to you? For even sinners love those who love them. If you do good to those who do good to you, what credit is that to you? For even sinners do the same. If you lend to those from whom you hope to receive, what credit is that to you? Even sinners lend to sinners, to receive as much again. But love your enemies, do good, and lend, expecting nothing in return. Your reward will be great, and you will be children of the Most High; for he is kind to the ungrateful and the wicked. Be merciful, just as your Father is merciful.'

(NRSV)

| Veronica Zundel

Reflection

This teaching is part of Luke's sermon on the plain, the equivalent of Matthew's sermon on the mount. Unlike Matthew, Luke includes not only blessings for those who endure suffering, but also curses on those who are rich, well fed and at ease. This is uncomfortable reading. Most people are happy to be generous to their friends, but Jesus wants us to go further – to give freely to those who make our lives hard.

The key is to become aware that this is how God has treated, and continues to treat, us. We the human race have ignored God, defied God, at times found God an unwelcome nuisance – in our treatment of Jesus, we have even killed God. God's response has been to keep loving us until we respond to that love.

Victorian philanthropists divided the objects of their charity into the 'deserving' and the 'undeserving' poor. Sometimes it seems that thinking is still prevalent in our society. But there is no such classification in God's mercy, nor should there be in ours. Our giving should be unreserved, for those we give to are just as human as we are.

When a lone gunman shot dead several schoolchildren at an Amish school and then shot himself, the community extended forgiveness and reached out to his widow and family. I think they were only able to do this because they had long practised forgiving and sharing with each other. Mercy is a habit to be learned.

> Keep your eyes open for how you can bless
> an 'enemy' today.

| Chris Pullenayegem

Too busy to love?

Luke 10:33–37

[Jesus said,] 'But a Samaritan, as he travelled, came where the man was; and when he saw him, he took pity on him. He went to him and bandaged his wounds, pouring on oil and wine. Then he put the man on his own donkey, brought him to an inn and took care of him. The next day he took out two denarii and gave them to the innkeeper. "Look after him," he said, "and when I return, I will reimburse you for any extra expense you may have." Which of these three do you think was a neighbour to the man who fell into the hands of robbers?' The expert in the law replied, 'The one who had mercy on him.' Jesus told him, 'Go and do likewise.' (NIV)

Reflection

This parable of Jesus is in response to a question, 'Who is my neighbour?', by a teacher of the Torah. Historically, there was no love lost between Samaritans and Jews. They despised each other. And yet, Jesus contrasts the action of the Samaritan to that of the two priests described earlier in the parable, who are not dissimilar to the questioner. The priest simply walked past the injured man, ignoring his obvious need. In a social experiment, a seminary found that 90% of seminarians did not stop to help someone in great distress even though they were on their way to finalise sermons on this very parable. A distressed person was placed in their pathway but urgency was created by the experimenters by suggesting that the seminarians were late for their class. In their context, perception of having limited time resulted in behaviours incongruent with their education and career: a calling to help others.

Loving our neighbour requires a sacrificial sharing of the resources of love. It means going out of our way, getting messy and it may even cost us financially, just like it did the Samaritan. It may also mean crossing cultural and racial boundaries, risking and putting other priorities and plans on hold. Think about what kind of world we would live in if we loved our neighbours as ourselves.

> God of love, give me the kind of love that knows
> no boundaries, is willing to go the distance and doesn't
> count the cost. Amen

| Chris Pullenayegem

God's order

Luke 12:29–34

'And do not set your heart on what you will eat or drink; do not worry about it. For the pagan world runs after all such things, and your Father knows that you need them. But seek his kingdom, and these things will be given to you as well. Do not be afraid, little flock, for your Father has been pleased to give you the kingdom. Sell your possessions and give to the poor. Provide purses for yourselves that will not wear out, a treasure in heaven that will never fail, where no thief comes near and no moth destroys. For where your treasure is, there your heart will be also.'

(NIV)

| Chris Pullenayegem

Reflection

Worry and anxiety seem to be epidemic these days, given the number of people who suffer from depression and feelings of isolation. The antidote to worry and anxiety is trust. But in this passage, Jesus seems to be taking that up a notch. He is asking us not just to trust God, Yahweh-jireh, our provider, but to understand that God's provision is not only for us and our use but also to be used to help others.

As we become channels of blessings to others, at least three things happen to us. First, we learn to hold 'things' lightly: see the temporal nature of all that is earthly. We realise that, whether it is our homes, finances or education, we are only stewards of the gifts that God has given us for tending. Second, our hearts develop the godly character of compassion, the sensitivity to see the needs of others through the eyes of Jesus. Third, the Spirit grows in us a desire to seek after not the material but God first, knowing that in doing this we are trusting in God's providential care over our lives. Seeking God first is a kingdom principle that puts balance and meaning into our lives, sets the tone of our worship, regulates our relationships with others and allows resources to be generously shared.

> Lord, take my heart and my life, and may they be fully consecrated to you this day. Let nothing or no one take your place in my heart today and forever. Amen

| Chris Pullenayegem

Investing for the future

Luke 16:5–8

> 'So he called in each one of his master's debtors. He asked the first, "How much do you owe my master?" "Three thousand litres of olive oil," he replied. The manager told him, "Take your bill, sit down quickly, and make it fifteen hundred." Then he asked the second, "And how much do you owe?" "Thirty tons of wheat," he replied. He told him, "Take your bill and make it twenty-four." The master commended the dishonest manager because he had acted shrewdly. For the people of this world are more shrewd in dealing with their own kind than are the people of the light.' (NIV)

| Chris Pullenayegem

Reflection

Read out of context, this parable seems un-Christian. What place does cheating (a.k.a shrewdness) have in the life of a follower of Jesus? Are we expected to be dishonest in dealing with others? In reality, Jesus is making a point about how we as believers are to exercise prudence in preparing for eternity. He is alerting us to the fact that we can be less careful about how we invest in our eternal future than secularly minded folk do in their temporal lives. 'Take a lesson,' he says, even from these dishonest wheeler-dealers.

That we make every effort to ensure that we are heavily invested into the future is the point of this parable. But what does investing into our eternal future look like, knowing that we cannot take anything with us when we transition? In similar parables, Jesus infers that our heart is the cradle of our desires, where our loyalties and priorities are nurtured. Thus preparing for eternity has to do with a) acquiring a long-term perspective of life; b) detaching ourselves from material deadweight; and c) aligning our hearts with God's purposes.

We live in a system that is geared for the here and now. A fast-food, drive-through mentality and instant gratification are values that characterise our society. And yet, we as Christ-followers are called to live with eternity in focus. How we do this could determine our witness, our character, our relationships and the way we share our resources.

> 'If any of you lacks wisdom, you should ask God, who gives generously to all without finding fault, and it will be given to you' (James 1:5).

| Chris Pullenayegem

Caught in the middle

Luke 16:10–13

'Whoever can be trusted with very little can also be trusted with much, and whoever is dishonest with very little will also be dishonest with much. So if you have not been trustworthy in handling worldly wealth, who will trust you with true riches? And if you have not been trustworthy with someone else's property, who will give you property of your own? No one can serve two masters. Either you will hate the one and love the other, or you will be devoted to the one and despise the other. You cannot serve both God and Money.'

(NIV)

| Chris Pullenayegem

Reflection

On the face of it, this passage seems to be about trustworthiness. It is, but that's not all; there is more. Jesus zeroes in on loyalty, the allegiance of the heart. Living in a dualistic frame of mind is possible at an intellectual level. It is possible to entertain two very divergent ideas and still function effectively. But matters concerning the heart are not the same. The heart can only have one master.

A gruesome but common form of torture or punishment used in the past was to tie individuals to horses, who were then forced to pull in opposite directions until their bodies ripped apart. Trying to serve both the true God and money produces a similar result: body and soul torn apart, a useless state of being. The good news is that loyalty to Jesus ensures us of a fulfilled and content life, his best for us, in our future and our present. The bad news is that allegiance to any other, especially money, though offering temporal pleasure, leads us down a slippery slope of discontentment and constant craving for the next best thing – until all we are is consumed by the insatiable need for love, acceptance and fulfilment that this 'other god' cannot give us. There is only one thing worse than choosing the latter: trying to serve both!

Jesus, save me from the folly of trying to follow you and the ways of the world. Teach me that following you helps me live life as it should be. Amen

Chris Pullenayegem

Rich man, poor man

Luke 16:22–25

'The time came when the beggar died and the angels carried him to Abraham's side. The rich man also died and was buried. In Hades, where he was in torment, he looked up and saw Abraham far away, with Lazarus by his side. So he called to him, "Father Abraham, have pity on me and send Lazarus to dip the tip of his finger in water and cool my tongue, because I am in agony in this fire." But Abraham replied, "Son, remember that in your lifetime you received your good things, while Lazarus received bad things, but now he is comforted here and you are in agony."'

(NIV)

Reflection

The first half of this parable describes the rich man ignoring the pleas of Lazarus the beggar. But in heaven, their roles are reversed. Is Jesus promoting the concept of karma or encouraging revenge-taking in this brief parable? Is it wrong to be wealthy? Do all rich people go to hell? No. In reality, this is an allegorical story that contrasts the condition of two very different categories of people – the rich and the poor in our world – and how they choose to share their resources. Jesus' criticism of the rich (which included the religious rulers at that time), who saw life as a zero-sum game ('if I win, you lose'), is aimed at those who hoard their wealth and place their wants and desires above everyone else's.

A selfish and self-centred lifestyle is consistently denounced in the scriptures and is antithetical to the lifestyle of a follower of Jesus. The purpose of wealth is not to feed the cravings of the rich but it is rather a resource to be distributed among those who are less fortunate. This is God's way of taking care of the weak, vulnerable and marginalised in our communities. The story is a stark reminder to all of us that what we have is not our own; it is simply entrusted to us for good stewarding, to be used for God's greater kingdom purposes. Our reluctance to share these gifts, an outflow of our self-centred condition, could be a prediction of where we could spend eternity: completely alienated from God's presence.

> Wealth can be acquired by anyone using any means. Christian character is built through faithful obedience to and application of God's word to our lives.

| Chris Pullenayegem

Small offering, large results

John 6:8–13

Another of his disciples, Andrew, Simon Peter's brother, spoke up, 'Here is a boy with five small barley loaves and two small fish, but how far will they go among so many?' Jesus said, 'Make the people sit down.' There was plenty of grass in that place, and they sat down (about five thousand men were there). Jesus then took the loaves, gave thanks, and distributed to those who were seated as much as they wanted. He did the same with the fish. When they had all had enough to eat, he said to his disciples, 'Gather the pieces that are left over. Let nothing be wasted.' So they gathered them and filled twelve baskets with the pieces of the five barley loaves left over by those who had eaten.

(NIV)

| Chris Pullenayegem

Reflection

Each actor in this story has a tale to tell – from worshipful awe to shock to cynical disbelief, depending on whom you asked. Today, we pick up the boy's story and reflect on the way he shared his resources. Imagine you were that boy. First of all, some ragged-looking men approach you and ask if they can borrow your lunch. Next, it's being passed to their even more ragged-looking leader, who does something strange to it. And before you know it, every-one is eating fish and barley loaves and the men are collecting baskets full of leftovers.

What if you had run away or refused, keeping what you had to yourself? Easy to do for many reasons: fear, feelings of inade-quacy, self-doubt and sometimes sheer stubbornness.

Thankfully, the boy did share what he had, and the miracle story reminds us that it's often the little things we have that get multi-plied and used a thousand times, if we are able to hand them over to God. Partnering with God doesn't mean that we need to show off; it's just that we need to give what we have, insignificant as it seems, trusting that Jesus will use it for his kingdom purposes. We all have a packed lunch waiting to be multiplied a thousand-fold. Will we hand it over?

> God, help me to realise that however small and insignificant my offering might seem, placed in the hands of Jesus, it could have a mind-blowing impact in your world.

| Chris Pullenayegem

Making sharing a lifestyle

Acts 4:32–35

All the believers were one in heart and mind. No one claimed that any of their possessions was their own, but they shared everything they had. With great power the apostles continued to testify to the resurrection of the Lord Jesus. And God's grace was so powerfully at work in them all that there was no needy person among them. For from time to time those who owned land or houses sold them, brought the money from the sales and put it at the apostles' feet, and it was distributed to anyone who had need. (NIV)

Reflection

The early church recognised the place of material resources – they were theirs not to own but to be stewarded and distributed in a way that advanced God's kingdom. 'There was no needy person among them' was a testament to their everyday faith and practice, and it exemplified Jesus' instruction that the way to save our lives is to lose it for his sake. There is blessing in giving, releasing, letting go of… It blesses the giver and the receiver and opens up channels of grace through which God's grace flows freely and powerfully.

More than the act (of giving), these accounts and other references in scripture remind us that the mindset or attitude of giving is even more important. When you truly love, you give. God demonstrated this by so loving the world that he gave his only Son. The early believers caught the fire. They understood that if their small movement was to grow, they had to do this together; that in sharing their resources, no one would be left behind; that each person had shared responsibility for the total well-being of the other.

Our world and our individualistic culture teaches us the opposite. And worse still, this mentality has invaded the church. We don't live in a world of scarce resources – they are just unequally distributed.

> Christians occupy seats at the highest levels of influence in government and business. Could we imagine a day when they would lead the way in creating a world where no one lived in need? In the meantime, what influence could you exert in your domains to help?

| Chris Pullenayegem

Holding back or holding on to?

Acts 5:1–4

Now a man named Ananias, together with his wife Sapphira, also sold a piece of property. With his wife's full knowledge he kept back part of the money for himself, but brought the rest and put it at the apostles' feet. Then Peter said, 'Ananias, how is it that Satan has so filled your heart that you have lied to the Holy Spirit and have kept for yourself some of the money you received for the land? Didn't it belong to you before it was sold? And after it was sold, wasn't the money at your disposal? What made you think of doing such a thing? You have not lied just to human beings but to God.'

(NIV)

| Chris Pullenayegem

Reflection

Ananias and his wife died having lied. Why did they keep back part of what they owned in the first place? What's wrong with giving only a part of your possessions to a common cause? Well, nothing – if that is what you are able to give.

In this passage, we encounter the church in its infancy. It had no political or commercial power, no influence and definitely no large membership making up the movement. The believers were busy looking after the interests of each other, especially making sure that no one was in need (materially) so that they could together, as a community, grow in the knowledge and love of Jesus. In this vulnerable state of growing, there was no room for compromise. Lies had no place. If left unchecked, Satan could have used this to torpedo and wreck the larger picture – a growing movement founded on trust, honesty and openness.

There's another lesson to be learned, too. The property that Ananias possessed did not ultimately belong to him. It belonged to God, the one who provides for us all. By holding back, Ananias had bought into the false assumption that he was the owner, not a steward, and that he could do with the property whatever he wished.

> What we have is given to us by God. It is ours not to dispose of selfishly but rather to be used for the greater good.

| Chris Pullenayegem

Blessing is in the journey

Acts 11:27–30

> During this time some prophets came down from Jerusalem to Antioch. One of them, named Agabus, stood up and through the Spirit predicted that a severe famine would spread over the entire Roman world. (This happened during the reign of Claudius.) The disciples, as each one was able, decided to provide help for the brothers and sisters living in Judea. This they did, sending their gift to the elders by Barnabas and Saul.
>
> (NIV)

Reflection

The book of Acts is replete with accounts of people helping people as an outcome of their newfound faith. This was one instance. A predicted famine, a need expressed – and believers jump right in to help by sharing resources as they are able. There were no relief agencies that would take care of food distribution, just people who loved God and God's people.

It's worth observing a few things in this account. The disciples recognised the voice of the Spirit, spoken through Agabus, and this faith led them to action. They were noticed for their generosity and their willingness to share and have 'all things in common'. Sharing has at least three benefits: it rightly adjusts our attitude towards possessions; it blesses the giver and the receiver; and it fosters trust and community.

Often the word 'blessing' is interpreted to mean material wealth, whether homes, vehicles, money in the bank, access to privileges, etc. Many proponents of the prosperity gospel, or 'blessing theology', preach that material wealth is an indication of God's favour and acceptance of our righteous lifestyles. Nothing is further from the truth. Using that yardstick, the apostles must have severely displeased God, since they all died as paupers, and many as martyrs! I believe that the blessing lies in the process God takes us through and the character building that ensues, especially while being tested though hardship, pain and suffering. Wealth, on the other hand, is not ours to hoard. It is God's resource, meant to be shared and used for kingdom-building purposes.

> God does not need us to accomplish his purposes. However, he invites us to partner in building the kingdom of God on earth by using our gifts and sharing our resources with the world.

| Chris Pullenayegem

Hospitality is an act of worship

Romans 12:10–13, 19–21

Be devoted to one another in love. Honour one another above yourselves. Never be lacking in zeal, but keep your spiritual fervour, serving the Lord. Be joyful in hope, patient in affliction, faithful in prayer. Share with the Lord's people who are in need. Practise hospitality... Do not take revenge, my dear friends, but leave room for God's wrath, for it is written: 'It is mine to avenge; I will repay,' says the Lord. On the contrary: 'If your enemy is hungry, feed him; if he is thirsty, give him something to drink. In doing this, you will heap burning coals on his head.' Do not be overcome by evil, but overcome evil with good. (NIV)

Reflection

Practise hospitality: two words that have enormous kingdom currency. Biblical hospitality validates all the other directives mentioned before it: devotion, honour, zeal, fervour, joy, patience, faithfulness, sharing and more. And to be clear, hospitality is not the same as entertainment. Rather, it's a place of vulnerability, a posture of inviting others to participate in each other's lives in ways that exemplifies what it is to be the body of Christ. It is an act of worship.

The Hebrew scriptures (the Old Testament) are packed with teaching about hospitality, especially towards strangers. Strangers would literally walk into your tent without warning, expecting to find food and shelter for the night.

Sharing coffee and biscuits in a coffee shop are good starts, but practising hospitality requires a different mindset. It requires a willingness to be exposed, to sacrifice and even to be exploited. As a community developer, I remember visiting a rural family in Asia, who invited our team into their 100-square-foot hut, insisting that we stay for lunch. Upon accepting their invitation, I noticed their son dart out of the house and return shortly with some vegetables and a live chicken. That meal would have cost half a month's wages and yet, they would rather be in debt than let us go hungry. It seems a universal reality that the less people have, the more they give.

> Lord, open my heart wide so that those strangers will feel welcome as they walk through the open door of hospitality into your warm and inviting presence.

George M. Wieland

Sharing across cultures

1 Corinthians 12:12–14

> Just as a body, though one, has many parts, but all its many parts form one body, so it is with Christ. For we were all baptised by one Spirit so as to form one body – whether Jews or Gentiles, slave or free – and we were all given the one Spirit to drink. Even so the body is not made up of one part but of many. (NIV)

| George M. Wieland

Reflection

To be in Christ is more than a theological idea. It is a real, lived relationship, not only with Christ but also with everyone else whom God's Spirit brings into that same life in Christ. It is no accident that the apostle Paul's most extensive description of the church as a body is found in this letter to the church in Corinth, which seems to have been beset with divisions and conflicts. Some of those disputes might have been over matters of belief or which leaders and teachers they most admired. The fundamental fault lines highlighted in today's reading, however, concern ethnic identity and socio-economic status.

We live at a time of heightened intercultural tensions and increasing social inequalities. In such an environment, it can be difficult even to imagine what a genuine sharing of life and resources between very different people would look like in practice. It was no easier at the time that the first messengers of good news made their way through the cities and towns of the Roman Empire. What the writers of the New Testament expected was nothing less than a countercultural miracle – a startlingly diverse community that offered visible witness to the transformation and reconciliation that God is accomplishing in Christ.

Yesterday, I had dinner with the pastor and a group of members of a local church here in Auckland, New Zealand. People who had come from China, Nigeria, Singapore, Korea, Japan, India, the Pacific, Chile, the USA and New Zealand met to share a meal, learn about each other and read the Bible together, and they sought to cooperate with what God is doing in bringing people from over 60 nations into one body and demonstrating the possibility of rich, authentic community in this hyper-diverse city.

> Ask God to show you fresh possibilities for the life
> and witness of a diverse community in Christ.

| George M. Wieland

Sharing with love

1 Corinthians 13:1–3

If I speak in the tongues of men or of angels, but do not have love, I am only a resounding gong or a clanging cymbal. If I have the gift of prophecy and can fathom all mysteries and all knowledge, and if I have a faith that can move mountains, but do not have love, I am nothing. If I give all I possess to the poor and give over my body to hardship that I may boast, but do not have love, I gain nothing. (NIV)

| George M. Wieland

Reflection

Really? Supernatural gifts and insight, great acts of faith, self-sacrificial giving, enduring extreme suffering – all this means nothing? That's what Paul says: nothing, without love. This is written to a church that seemed to prize such manifestations as measures of spiritual achievement and status, while at the same time tearing the community of believers apart with destructive rivalries, cruel criticism and the refusal to accept other Jesus-followers who did not belong to their group or practise their faith in quite the same way. Paul's point is not that those practices could never have any value. He has just provided a catalogue of gifts and ways of serving that include all those cited here, with an appeal to exercise them fully and eagerly so that God's grace may be shared. He is not saying, 'Don't do any of those things – instead, just love each other.' Rather, his meaning is, 'Do these things, but ensure that you are doing them with love.'

Without love, any speaking, doing, giving or sharing can be self-serving. Spectacular gifts can be exercised in a way that grabs attention or dominates; claims to special insight can be used to wield power over others; giving can be an attempt to control. But when exercised with love, all of those things serve their purpose, as means whereby good comes to others and the body of Christ is built up.

Mother Teresa, honoured for her selfless devotion to the poorest of the poor in Kolkata, is reputed to have said, 'Not all of us can do great things, but we can do small things with great love.'

> What am I currently doing with little love? What would be different if I did it with great love?

George M. Wieland

Sharing cheerfully

2 Corinthians 9:6–9, 13

Remember this: whoever sows sparingly will also reap sparingly, and whoever sows generously will also reap generously. Each of you should give what you have decided in your heart to give, not reluctantly or under compulsion, for God loves a cheerful giver. And God is able to bless you abundantly, so that in all things at all times, having all that you need, you will abound in every good work. As it is written: 'They have freely scattered their gifts to the poor; their righteousness endures forever'... Because of the service by which you have proved yourselves, others will praise God for the obedience that accompanies your confession of the gospel of Christ, and for your generosity in sharing with them and with everyone else. (NIV)

Reflection

There are delightful word-pictures in this passage. The image of the sower is familiar from Jesus' parables. This is not the gardener meticulously measuring a few vegetable seeds into neatly drilled holes. It is the peasant farmer hefting a great basketful of seed as he moves through the ploughed field, casting fistfuls to the left and the right. It is this vivid image of 'scattering abroad' that Paul wants to hold before his readers as he asks them to participate in God's provision for people in need in another part of the world.

In contrast to a grudging, miserly stance, Paul commends giving 'on the basis of blessing' (the phrase that the NIV renders 'generously'). This is giving that both springs out of blessings received and is directed towards bestowing blessing, not merely meeting an obligation. Similarly, when God gives, it is 'abundant', spilling over, more than enough; and our giving is to be of the same character.

Paul reminds them that God loves a 'cheerful' giver. The term there is *hilaros*, from which is derived the English word 'hilarity'. What would hilarious generosity look like? This certainly describes God's giving towards us and, to the extent that our giving carries forward that overspill of God's grace, glorifies God and demonstrates our alignment with the gospel.

From what does the gospel need to set me free, so that my giving to others will reflect God's extravagant generosity?

| George M. Wieland

Sharing in responsibility

Galatians 6:1–6

Brothers and sisters, if someone is caught in a sin, you who live by the Spirit should restore that person gently. But watch yourselves, or you also may be tempted. Carry each other's burdens, and in this way you will fulfil the law of Christ. If anyone thinks they are something when they are not, they deceive themselves. Each one should test their own actions. Then they can take pride in themselves alone, without comparing themselves to someone else, for each one should carry their own load. Nevertheless, the one who receives instruction in the word should share all good things with their instructor.

(NIV)

| George M. Wieland

Reflection

The life of the church calls for responsibility: corporate and individual, for others and for oneself. In the original language, some of the instructions in this passage are plural, others singular. We could set them out like this: 'You people (plural), restore anyone who has slipped up; each of you (singular), watch yourself that you're not tempted. You people (plural), take up each other's burdens and thus fulfil Christ's law; each of you (singular), scrutinise your own work and take up your own obligation.'

The church is addressed as family ('brothers and sisters') and people led by the Spirit. When someone in this community is found to be falling or stepping away from the right path, the family has to step up. The term translated 'restore' is the word used for mending a net. It is not only the struggling individual who has to be 'mended'; the church itself needs to be 'mended' by the recovery of that person to full participation in its life. The goal is restoration, and the character of the community's response is to be gentleness, a fruit of the Spirit (Galatians 5:22–23).

Interestingly, the instruction to share good things with your teacher is also singular. Individuals are being urged to recognise that they owe a debt to those from whom they are taught God's message, and to take their share of the responsibility for partnering with them so that they can perform that ministry.

In what area – personal or communal, for yourself or for others – could or should you step up and take more responsibility? What will that mean in practice?

| George M. Wieland

Sharing good, not bad

Ephesians 4:28–32

Anyone who has been stealing must steal no longer, but must work, doing something useful with their own hands, that they may have something to share with those in need. Do not let any unwholesome talk come out of your mouths, but only what is helpful for building others up according to their needs, that it may benefit those who listen. And do not grieve the Holy Spirit of God, with whom you were sealed for the day of redemption. Get rid of all bitterness, rage and anger, brawling and slander, along with every form of malice. Be kind and compassionate to one another, forgiving each other, just as in Christ God forgave you.

(NIV)

| George M. Wieland

Reflection

'I'm angry with God; he keeps letting me down.' Such sentiments are not uncommon, but the reason that the young man gave was more surprising: 'I have a problem with stealing. I asked God to stop me but he hasn't, so now I've lost my job.' As a young pastor, my mind went to the command, 'Anyone who has been stealing must steal no longer.' Straightforward! But for Paul, there is more at play here than an individual's responsibility to change his or her behaviour. These instructions are framed within the shared life of a community. The concern is not only with an individual's moral rectitude but even more with the community that the individual's actions, words and attitudes will either harm or help.

Furthermore, the guidance is not in the form of a stark list of un-related dos and don'ts. It is a series of contrasting options: not stealing but sharing with others; not talk that corrupts but words that benefit others; not poisonous feelings and behaviour but kindness, compassion and forgiveness for others. For good or for ill, we are all continually sharing something by our actions, words and attitudes. This reading urges us not merely to restrain from anything that is destructive but to choose and cultivate in its place behaviours, words and attitudes that will bless and build up the community of which we are part.

In what specific matter do you want to choose the better way? What will be the effect on others and on your communities (church, home, workplace, etc.) as a whole?

| George M. Wieland

Sharing humbly

Philippians 2:1–4

Therefore if you have any encouragement from being united with Christ, if any comfort from his love, if any common sharing in the Spirit, if any tenderness and compassion, then make my joy complete by being like-minded, having the same love, being one in spirit and of one mind. Do nothing out of selfish ambition or vain conceit. Rather, in humility value others above yourselves, not looking to your own interests but each of you to the interests of the others.

(NIV)

Reflection

I was at an army camp to support a friend who was being commissioned as a chaplain. An imposing lieutenant colonel strode forward to read the Bible passage selected by my friend for the occasion, Philippians 2:1–11. He got as far as verse 3: 'In humility regard others as better than yourselves' (NRSV). There was a pause. 'I must admit I have a problem with that one,' he said, and carried on with the reading. Laughter and knowing looks confirmed that humility was not a trait many of those present associated with their camp commander. He was used to looking down on others from above, whether soldiers whom he had the authority to command or an enemy whom he was mandated to defeat. That kind of leadership seems to require assertiveness, pride and a stance of superiority.

The way of Jesus could not be more different. His is servant leadership, letting go of privilege, position, possessions and pride, adopting the servant's role and ultimately giving his life for others (vv. 5–11). The love, unity in the Spirit and shared orientation and purpose that our reading commends are only possible when the members of the community are joined to Christ to the extent that their lives take on that same pattern. We are called to follow Jesus in his intentional downward mobility from a place of superiority and control to a place of humility and surrender of our self-interest. From there, we, like Jesus, can look up at others and see them as people to be valued, loved and served: people with whom we are to share our lives and resources with humility.

> Picture yourself kneeling down and from that position looking up at the members of your church or group or the staff that you manage or lead. How do you see them? And how will you serve them?

| George M. Wieland

Sharing between poor and rich

1 Timothy 6:17–19

> Command those who are rich in this present world not to be arrogant nor to put their hope in wealth, which is so uncertain, but to put their hope in God, who richly provides us with everything for our enjoyment. Command them to do good, to be rich in good deeds, and to be generous and willing to share. In this way they will lay up treasure for themselves as a firm foundation for the coming age, so that they may take hold of the life that is truly life. (NIV)

| George M. Wieland

Reflection

God has designed an ecosystem of grace, whereby God's provision flows through those who are entrusted with the means to help and reach others who are looking to God in their need. What obstructs this flow of provision? The passage exposes aspects of the problem: arrogance on the part of the rich, trusting in wealth instead of in God, choosing accumulation of things for themselves over sharing true life in community with others. Interestingly, those negative traits of the rich contrast markedly with the positive characteristics of another group of people in this letter. These are dependence on God, habitual practical goodness and devotion to serving others. Who exhibits those qualities? Widows without family support, the most vulnerable people in that society (1 Timothy 5:3, 5, 10). The rich are to learn faith, generosity and service from the poor.

Teaching in Nepal, I was startled by shrieks of anguish. A heavy door had slammed shut, jamming a young man's hand. He was screaming in pain, fingers misshapen and discoloured. I knew the college had no first aid kit, but I had some paracetamol. 'Wait,' I said, 'I'll get medicine.' 'Sir,' replied a young female student, 'thank you for your medicine, but we want you to pray.' Somewhat chastened, I prayed. When I opened my eyes, he held up an apparently undamaged hand, smiled and told me the pain was gone. My gift to them was going to be a tiny share in the medical resources of the rich; their gift to me was the faith of the poor.

> What holds you back from sharing what you have with others who need it? What do you need them to share with you?

George M. Wieland

Sharing faith-in-action

James 2:14–18

What good is it, my brothers and sisters, if someone claims to have faith but has no deeds? Can such faith save them? Suppose a brother or a sister is without clothes and daily food. If one of you says to them, 'Go in peace; keep warm and well fed,' but does nothing about their physical needs, what good is it? In the same way, faith by itself, if it is not accompanied by action, is dead. But someone will say, 'You have faith; I have deeds.' Show me your faith without deeds, and I will show you my faith by my deeds. (NIV)

| George M. Wieland

Reflection

Faith has several aspects. These include belief about, trust in and faithfulness to God. In today's passage, faith is claimed by someone who can offer no practical demonstration of it. James applies one simple test: what do you do when you encounter a member of the family of faith in dire practical need?

If the claim to have faith refers to true belief, it is reasonable to expect behaviour that reflects what is believed about God. To speak words of blessing over someone in desperate need, while heading off and leaving them in their plight, displays either callous indifference or a desire to protect oneself from the discomfort of sitting with them in their situation. Is that really how they believe God sees, speaks and acts?

If it is confident trust that is affirmed, how does that correspond to the apparent inability to risk an act of generosity and love? If they are asserting their faithfulness to God, how could they so heedlessly disregard the commandment that encapsulates all that God seeks: to love God and neighbour?

A further dimension to faith is that of being 'in the faith', part of the believing community. Someone who can glibly pass over the extreme suffering of another member of that family and fob them off with a platitude must question the genuineness of their own belonging to it.

> Think of an occasion when you have become aware of a brother or sister in extreme need and have felt an inner resistance to helping them. Which aspect of your faith was being challenged? Pray that God will increase your faith.

| George M. Wieland

Sharing in God's nature

2 Peter 1:3–7

His divine power has given us everything we need for a godly life through our knowledge of him who called us by his own glory and goodness. Through these he has given us his very great and precious promises, so that through them you may participate in the divine nature, having escaped the corruption in the world caused by evil desires. For this very reason, make every effort to add to your faith goodness; and to goodness, knowledge; and to knowledge, self-control; and to self-control, perseverance; and to perseverance, godliness; and to godliness, mutual affection; and to mutual affection, love. (NIV)

| George M. Wieland

Reflection

The astonishing thought in this passage is that God wants to share God's very nature with us, and calls people everywhere not to do their best to become acceptable but to draw near and have their lives infused with God's character and power. Faith orients us towards God and what God promises. Peter was writing to Gentile followers of Jesus in environments where characteristics such as self-control, godliness and selfless love for others were neither pervasive nor necessarily valued. But those who had come to know Jesus (v. 8) yearned to leave behind those behaviours that destroyed them and others and to move towards a new vision of goodness found in sharing the life of God. The qualities listed in our reading are not a ladder to climb to arrive at the life of God; they are themselves a sharing in that life.

I had access to exercise machines and weights, a training programme and dietary advice. I had everything I needed for a healthy life, and great and precious promises of fitness. My wife had gifted me a gym subscription. But were these promises fulfilled? Not entirely. There was nothing lacking in the provision, but there was deficiency in the 'making every effort' component. Feed unholy habits and they will devour us; practise the holy habits and they will grow us into fuller life in God.

> Identify one of those qualities that you need to grow in. Ponder the promise of sharing in God's nature and the provision God has made for that. What specific effort, in relation to that quality, will you seek God's help to make this week?

George M. Wieland

Sharing love-in-action

1 John 3:16–18

> This is how we know what love is: Jesus Christ laid down his life for us. And we ought to lay down our lives for our brothers and sisters. If anyone has material possessions and sees a brother or sister in need but has no pity on them, how can the love of God be in that person? Dear children, let us not love with words or speech but with actions and in truth.
>
> (NIV)

| George M. Wieland

Reflection

I was a child when pictures of unimaginable suffering in Biafra's civil war and subsequent famine hit British television screens in 1967. Such things had happened before, but for the first time the world was looking on. Like countless others, I was jolted into action, eager to make my small contribution to alleviating such suffering. In the UK, thousands of Christians sent money to the Evangelical Alliance, which at that time did not have a mechanism for delivering aid. To channel this outpouring of generosity, the Evangelical Alliance Relief Fund was formed.

Today, Tearfund and other such organisations struggle with donors' compassion fatigue, a dampening of the emotional response to suffering. We have seen so much, and with the tap of a screen we can select images and reports from any number of horrendous situations. It takes a lot to provoke anything approaching the breadth and urgency of those responses half a century ago.

John's challenge to those who lack pity therefore stings many of us. What he is talking about, however, is more than an emotional response over which we may have little control. The test is set out step by step: if we have learned from Jesus that love is enacted in self-giving for others; if we have the means to help; if we see a brother or sister in need; what do we do then? The expression 'has no pity' is more literally 'locks their heart against them'. The heart locked against a brother or sister in need cannot at the same time be open to the inflow of the love of God.

> What in me is resisting the flow of God's love-in-action through me to someone whom I have the means to help? How can that blockage be cleared?

Whole-church resources

MISSIONAL DISCIPLESHIP RESOURCES FOR CHURCHES

Individual copy £4.99

Holy Habits is an adventure in Christian discipleship. Inspired by Luke's model of church found in Acts 2:42–47, it identifies ten habits and encourages the development of a way of life formed by them. These resources are designed to help churches explore the habits creatively in a range of contexts and live them out in whole-life, intergenerational, missional discipleship.

HOLY**HABITS**

These new additions to the Holy Habits resources have been developed to help churches and individuals explore the Holy Habits through prayerful engagement with the Bible and live them out in whole-life, missional discipleship.

Bible Reflections Edited by Andrew Roberts | Individual copy £3.99

Each set of Bible reading notes contains eight weeks of devotional material. Four writers bring different perspectives on the habit in question through their reflections on passages drawn from across the Bible narrative.

Group Studies Edited by Andrew Roberts | Individual copy £6.99

Each leader's guide contains eight sessions of Bible study material, providing off-the-peg material to help churches get started or continue with Holy Habits. Each session includes a Bible passage, reflections, group questions, community/outreach ideas, art and media links and a prayer.

Find out more at holyhabits.org.uk
and brfonline.org.uk/collections/holy-habits
Download a leaflet for your church leadership at
brfonline.org.uk/holyhabitsdownload

Are you looking to continue the habit of daily Bible reading?

With a subscription to BRF Bible reading notes, you'll have everything you need to nourish your relationship with the Bible and with God.

Our most popular and longest running series, *New Daylight*, features daily readings and reflections from a selection of much-beloved writers, dealing with a variety of themes and Bible passages. With the relevant passage printed alongside the comment, *New Daylight* is a practical and effective way of reading the Bible as a part of your everyday routine.

New Daylight is available in print, deluxe (large print), by email and as an app for iOS and Android.

'I think Bible reading notes are really underrated. At any age – there I was as a teenager getting as much out of them then as I am now – so they're for every age group, not just the very young and the very old. I think to have them as your bedside companion is a really wise idea throughout life.'

Debbie Thrower, Pioneer of BRF's Anna Chaplaincy programme

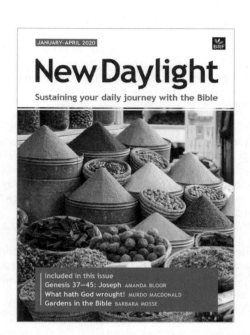

Also available:

Find out more at brfonline.org.uk

Praise for the original Holy Habits resources

'Here are some varied and rich resources to help further deepen our discipleship of Christ, encouraging and enabling us to adopt the life-transforming habits that make for following Jesus.'
Revd Dr Martyn Atkins, Team Leader & Superintendent Minister, Methodist Central Hall, Westminster

'The Holy Habits resources will help you, your church, your fellowship group, to engage in a journey of discovery about what it really means to be a disciple today. I know you will be encouraged, challenged and inspired as you read and work your way through… There is lots to study together and pray about, and that can only be good as our churches today seek to bring about the kingdom of God.'
Revd Loraine Mellor, President of the Methodist Conference 2017/18

'The Holy Habits resources help weave the spiritual through everyday life. They're a great tool that just get better with use. They help us grow in our desire to follow Jesus as their concern is formation not simply information.'
Olive Fleming Drane and John Drane

'The Holy Habits resources are an insightful and comprehensive manual for living in the way of Jesus in the 21st century: an imaginative, faithful and practical gift for the church that will sustain and invigorate our life and mission in a demanding world. The Holy Habits resources are potentially transformational for a church.'
Revd Ian Adams, Mission Spirituality Adviser for Church Mission Society

'To understand the disciplines of the Christian life without practising them habitually is like owning a fine collection of soap but never having a wash. The team behind Holy Habits knows this, which is why they have produced these excellent and practical resources. Use them, and by God's grace you will grow in holiness.'
Paul Bayes, Bishop of Liverpool